THREE

KINDS

OF

FAITH

FOR HEALING

(and as a bonus, several other kinds)

Bill Banks

Three Kinds Of Faith For Healing, Bill Banks
ISBN # 0-89228-103-3

Copyright © 1992
by IMPACT BOOKS, INC.
137 W. Jefferson, Kirkwood, Mo. 63122

Cover Design   - S P B Studios

DEDICATION

I dedicate this little book to Jesus Christ who by His grace healed me more than twenty years ago and has continued to draw me to a deeper relationship with Him.

And to the Holy Spirit who by His sweet grace, gifts and loving enablements continues doing the same works that Jesus did, which He said were the works of the Father.

> "But Jesus answered them, My Father worketh hitherto, and I work."
>
> John 5:17
>
> "If I do not the works of my Father, believe me not."
>
> John 10:37
>
> "Believest thou not that I am in the Father, and the Father in me? the words that I speak unto you I speak not of myself: but the Father that dwelleth in me, he doeth the works."
>
> John 14:10

Thus to our loving, compassionate Triune God, I humbly dedicate this effort with the prayer that it will bring light to those who still sit in darkness concerning the healing which Jesus has purchased for His people.

"For this people's heart is waxed gross, and their ears are dull of hearing, and their eyes they have closed; lest at any time they should see with their eyes and hear with their ears, and should understand with their heart, and should be converted, and I should heal them."

Matt.13:15 (cf Isa. 6:10)

CONTENTS

INTRODUCTION 7

1 THREE KINDS OF FAITH
   FOR HEALING................................9

2 *SEEKING FAITH* 15

3 *INTERCESSORY FAITH* 17

4 *MINISTRY FAITH* 23

5 *ELDER, OR BODY FAITH* 29

6 MERCY, GRACE, OR MIRACLE
   HEALINGS 35

   A Veteran Who Chose Hell......................40
   A Veteran Who Chose Heaven 44

7 THE PERSEVERANCE OF DANIEL...53

8 CLOSING THOUGHTS FOR THOSE
   NOT HEALED (YET!)....................63

SOME OF MY FAVORITE
HEALING SCRIPTURES................67

INTRODUCTION

Many today have been taught that the only way to really get healed is to personally have faith for our healing. We must, it is implied, somehow 'work up' or develop enough personal *faith-to-be-healed,* and then we will be healed. The implication is that our personal faith is the coin of the realm, and it will in some manner purchase our healing.

Jesus, we are repeatedly told in the Scriptures, was motivated to heal by compassion. Unfortunately in our day we often hear evangelists or ministers blame the lack of healing upon the poor victim of disease, by telling them that the reason they haven't been healed is because, "You don't have enough faith." I have know of some who were told, "the reason you people weren't healed tonight, is because there weren't enough hundred dollar bills in the offering plate!"

Such statements in addition to being utterly devoid of compassion, are terribly devastating to the poor hearers. One could never imagine Jesus saying something so heartless. Yet the same things are often said today. In addition, even those who have not heard the words spoken aloud have received them through implication from proud, spiritually 'superior' friends who believe that these sick individuals are somehow deficient in faith. Some because of what they have read have heaped similar condemnation upon themselves. These poor sick sheep for whom Jesus died, are living under the pain of condemnation in addition to the discomfort of their disease.

There is good news both for them and for us, because that teaching is wrong. There are more ways of being healed than just the one way, as we have been taught.

One day about twenty years ago I began sharing these revelations that I felt I'd received from the Lord concerning the three kinds of faith for healing with Derek Prince. He interrupted me and said, "Don't tell me any more than you already have. What you're saying is so good that I am apt to inadvertently steal it and use it myself."

Those kind words of encouragement from a man whom I considered to be one of the most anointed Bible teachers of our era, certainly boosted my faith in what I'd discovered. I have been further encouraged by the response every time I have shared this teaching. It is a great source of joy to see people's faces suddenly light up as these truths dawn upon their hearts.

Now, I want to share these truths with you, just the way the Lord showed them to me, so you can learn from the same situations and interpret the truths contained in them for yourself.

1

THREE KINDS OF FAITH

FOR HEALING

Anyone who tries to teach that there is only *one* way to obtain healing or only one kind of faith for healing is in error: Jesus, Himself, proves that. Jesus ministered to the problem of blindness, in at least *five* different ways:

Once with *spit*.. By applying spittle to the eyes of the blind person (Mark 8:22-26),

Once with *clay*.. Made by mixing spit and dust of the earth, and applying the clay to the eyes of the blind person (John 9:1ff),

Once with a *word*.. Jesus simply spoke the words "receive thy sight" and sight was restored (Luke 18:35-43),

Once with a *touch*.. "..Jesus had compassion on them and touched their eyes..." (Matthew 20:30-34),

Once with *deliverance*.. By casting out a spirit of blindness. (Matthew 12:22-24).

Thus, recorded in the Scriptures Jesus, Himself, ministered in at least *five different ways* to the problem of blindness. He was, and is, creative and knows exactly the right way to minister to the exact needs of individuals at the level of their spiritual as well as their physical need.

Some also teach that we cannot pray more than one time for the same need without somehow offending God, negating our first prayer, or of becoming faithless. Once again, this is not necessarily so, as the Lord showed me many years ago, while we were praying one winter evening for healing in the basement cafeteria of a large church. I had given my testimony of how the Lord Jesus Christ healed me of terminal cancer after the doctors had given me thirty-one blood transfusions and only forty-eight hours to live.[1]

After I finished my testimony, I invited those desiring healing to come forward for prayer. We prayed for dozens of people and saw most of them healed instantly. Then, finally the last one, a young woman with a spinal birth defect came and sat in the chair provided for the candidates for prayer. She stated that she had had minor discomfort throughout her life and was, in fact, in pain as she sat in the chair.

We prayed for her once; she was bettered but not completely healed. So, we prayed again, and she was still better, but not quite free of pain. We prayed the third time... and she was completely healed.

Since the hour was late and she was the last one needing prayer, I started for the corner of the room to get my

----

1. The story of the author's miraculous healing from terminal cancer is told in the book, *Alive Again!*

coat and hat to leave. Suddenly, I noticed out of the corner of my eye, a huge fellow charging across the room towards me. His face was a deep red, and I almost thought I could see steam coming out of his ears.

Nearing me, he bellowed, "How dare you do that?"

"Do what? I innocently asked, unaware of having done anything potentially offensive.

"How dare you pray for that woman - *three times*?" His voice rising to a shout. "I've read all the books on faith, and they say that it's wrong to pray more than one time *for anything*, that you negate your first prayer by praying the second time, that you insult God by your lack of faith that he heard you the first time."

Somewhat taken aback, I did not have a good answer for him. All I could muster was, "Well, Brother, all I can tell you is that it worked."

"I know that it worked and that's what makes me mad!" He said a little more softly. "My theology must be wrong."

I praise God for this man's willingness to learn when confronted by the facts. Many unfortunately are not.

As is so often the case, I learn more from my failures than from my apparent successes. A week later the Lord showed me in the Word of God, the answers that I should have given to my irately perplexed brother. I remembered that Paul had prayed more than once for a particular problem, and that like the Lord, he had also encouraged believers to "pray without ceasing." (I Thess. 5:17)

11

I also remembered the Lord Jesus's own encouragement to his followers to be like the friend who went at midnight seeking bread for a friend of his (Luke 11:5,ff), and his conclusion "to ask, seek, and knock" with the Greek tense indicating continuing action. However, the clearest answer for me was the one which the Holy Spirit quickened to my mind, in response to my prayerfully continuing to question Him about this issue. He gave to me an instance in Scripture when *Jesus, Himself, ministered more than one time for a healing!* Can it really be that Jesus had to minister more than one time for some one to be completely healed? Yes in Mark 8:22-25. Jesus was asked to minister to a blind man near Bethsaida.

> "And he cometh to Bethsaida; and they bring a blind man unto Him, and besought Him to touch him. And he took the blind man by the hand, and led him out of the town; and when he had spit on his eyes, and put his hands upon him, he asked him if he saw ought. And he looked up, and said, I see men as trees, walking. After that He put his hands again upon his eyes, and made him look up: and he was restored, and saw every man clearly."
>
> (Mark 8:22-25)

After Jesus had ministered to the man the first time by spitting on his eyes and laying on of his hands, He asked him if he could see. The man's response was that he could now "see men as trees, walking." (i.e. He was actually partially healed of blindness at this point.) A partial healing by Jesus? Albeit only a brief, temporary period of delay, another theological bubble is burst.

Jesus's actions in this case are very enlightening. He did not accept the partial healing as being the will of God; He did not accept the partial healing as sufficient; He did not criticize the man for lacking faith. He did not tell the man to, "Just claim it, brother!" Nor any of the other things we so often hear today, and might have expected Him to say if the current teachings were correct.

Instead Jesus continued ministering to the man! After the partial healing, Jesus laid his hands on the man a second time, and then made him look up. His sight was restored completely! He could see "every man clearly."

Jesus, whose faith was perfect both times that he ministered to the man, laid his hands upon the blind man twice, and ministered to him twice!

This account is a scriptural precedent for praying for someone more than one time!

OBSERVATION:

Certainly this truth should not be taken to the other extreme and be assumed to justify another common problem, the opposite swing of the pendulum, primarily among Pentecostal people, of being prayed for every time that there is a prayer line for healing, or every time that a new ministry passes through town. In my experience this seems to indicate a faith not in Jesus, the Healer, but rather a faith in someone or something new, i.e. having faith in someone else's faith, rather than seeking Jesus directly and individually. This is, no doubt, due to poor teaching and laziness (of which many of the rest of us may also be guilty). They are looking for an easier or quicker way of being healed than having to pay the price of seeking God on their own and expending the time and effort in personal prayer, which is often required.

It is not the goal of this writing to criticize others who have beautifully put forth a part of the truth of the gospel of healing, but rather this is offered to add insight, balance, and new dimensions of truth which have been granted to us by the Holy Spirit. I share them with you that the Body of Christ might be edified, and the church further equipped to defeat Satan's kingdom, to pull down his strongholds of sickness, pain and affliction.

=======

The Lord has revealed there are at least three main types of faith for healing illustrated in Scripture, and a fourth which is a combination of the other three. There may be even more, but I can now only share and testify of the truths which I have seen. Incidentally, it is an excellent discipline and challenge to study the healing accounts in the gospels to see into which of these four categories they fall.

I have come to see the following truths over a period of more than twenty years of involvement in the ministry of healing. These have now stood the test of time and have served to open the eyes of many both literally and spiritually over those years.

The first kind of faith for healing is that with which we are most familiar and which I shall call *seeking faith.*

14

2

SEEKING FAITH

Seeking faith is that faith manifested by the sick or afflicted person himself in determining to seek out Jesus on his own that he might receive a healing.

There are many examples of this type of faith for healing in the gospels. Two typical examples are to be found in the ninth chapter of Matthew. The first is that of two blind men,

> "And when Jesus departed thence, two blind men followed him, crying, and saying, Thou son of David, have mercy on us. And when he was come into the house, the blind men came to him: and Jesus saith unto them, *Believe ye* that I am able to do this? They said unto him, Yea, Lord. Then touched he their eyes, saying, According to *your faith* be it unto you. And their eyes were opened.."
>
> (Matthew 9:27-30a)

Here is recorded the account of two blind men healed when they personally sought Jesus and received a touch from Him which gave them sight. Jesus then spoke these words unto them, "according to *your faith* be it unto you." He thus placed the focus on their own *seeking faith* as the active ingredient producing their healing.

Also recorded in this chapter is perhaps the most familiar example of *seeking faith,* that of the woman with the flow of blood. She, on her own behalf, by a decision of her own will, sought out Jesus and determined to touch Him. She conveyed herself into his presence, touched the hem of his garment, and was thus made whole by His virtuous power. He, then addressed her with these enlightening words, "Daughter, be of good comfort; *thy faith* hath made thee whole." Again in this instance, Jesus focused upon her faith as the activating ingredient.

> "And, behold, a woman, which was diseased with an issue of blood twelve years, came behind him, and touched the hem of his garment: for she said within herself, if I may but touch his garment, I shall be whole. But Jesus turned him about, and when he saw her, he said, Daughter, be of good comfort; *thy faith* hath made thee whole. And the woman was made whole from that hour."
> Matthew 9:20-22

Although *seeking faith* is perhaps the most commonly observed type of faith for healing there are others. The next is *intercessory faith.*

16

3

INTERCESSORY FAITH

Intercessory faith for healing is that form of faith manifested by someone else in behalf of the person who is ill in order to bring them or their need to the attention of Jesus. Parents exemplified this type of faith in the scriptural accounts who came in behalf of their children, who could not come themselves. The children could not manifest faith for themselves; at least one of them was even dead by the time that the parent's request reached Jesus.

> "While he spake these things unto them, behold, there came a certain ruler, and worshipped him, saying, *My daughter is even now dead:* but come and lay thy hand upon her, and she shall live."
>
> Matthew 9:18

Every parent's request for the healing of a child was acknowledged and fulfilled. Their intercession and *intercessory faith* achieved the desired effect: healing from Jesus dispatched to the one in need. The account continues:

"While he yet spake, there came from the ruler of the synagogue's house certain which said, Thy daughter is dead: why troublest thou the Master any further? As soon as Jesus heard the word that was spoken, he saith unto the ruler of the synagogue, Be not afraid, only believe. And he suffered no man to follow him, save Peter, and James, and John the brother of James. And he cometh to the house of the ruler of the synagogue, and seeth the tumult, and them that wept and wailed greatly. And when he was come in, he saith unto them, Why make ye this ado, and weep? The damsel is not dead, but sleepeth. And they laughed him to scorn. But when *he had put them all out,* he taketh the father and the mother of the damsel, and them that were with him, and entereth in where the damsel was lying. And he took the damsel by the hand, and said unto her, Talitha cumi[1]; which is, being interpreted, Damsel, I say unto thee, arise. And straightway the damsel arose, and walked; for she was of the age of twelve years. And they were astonished with a great astonishment. And he charged them straitly that no man should know it; and commanded that something should be given her to eat."

Mark 5:35-43

----

1. These very words *Talitha cumi* were recorded in the ancient, original names of the stars. The amazing and faith-building gospel of Jesus Christ is recorded in those names and the message is unfolded in the book, *The Heavens Declare...* by the same author.

Luke in his rendering adds a significant detail to this account. "He suffered no man to go in, save Peter, and James, and John, and the father and the mother of the maiden."

Notice that Jesus put out all the doubters and those bewailing her death, all who could not see beyond death's hold. *Jesus artificially raised the level of faith* in the room before raising the girl from the dead!

OBSERVATION:

If you are seeking healing, turn your ears off to the doubters; endeavor to eliminate in so far as is possible all doubt. Also, if possible, immerse yourself in like-minded fellowship.

=======

This principle of *intercessory faith* is best exemplified by another familiar case, the man taken with palsy, who was carried by four friends to the house where Jesus was conducting a 'healing service.' Luke gives an account of the incident:

> "And, behold, men brought in a bed a man which was taken with a palsy: and they sought means to bring him in, and to lay him before him. And when they could not find by what way they might bring him in because of the multitude, they went upon the housetop, and let him down through the tiling with his couch into the midst before Jesus. And when he saw *their faith,* he said unto him, Man, thy sins are forgiven thee. And the scribes and the Pharisees

began to reason, saying, Who is this which speaketh blasphemies? Who can forgive sins, but God alone? But when Jesus perceived their thoughts, he answering said unto them, What reason ye in your hearts? Whether is easier, to say, thy sins be forgiven thee; or to say, Rise up and walk? But that ye may know that the Son of man hath power upon earth to forgive sins, (he said unto the sick of the palsy,) I say unto thee, Arise, and take up thy couch, and go into thine house. And immediately he rose up before them, and took up that whereon he lay, and departed to his own house, glorifying God. And they were all amazed, and they glorified God, and were filled with fear, saying, We have seen strange things to day."

Luke 5:18-26

The four friends, when they found that they were unable to gain entry to the house because of the great crowd, carried the man upon his pallet up to the roof. They took up the roofing material and lowered him down through the hole in the roof which they had created, so that the man was let down right in front of Jesus. *Their efforts brought his need to the attention of, and into the presence of, Jesus!*

Once again Jesus' actions and words interpret the situation and offer understanding. Jesus, as each of the first three gospel writers all record, took note of the *friends' faith.* "And when he saw *their faith..*" He said to the man on the pallet, *"Thy sins are forgiven thee."* A moment later he also said to him, *"Arise, and take up thy couch..."*

The point that must not be missed here is that Jesus saw *their faith*, not the afflicted man's faith. He saw the faith *of the men on the roof,* not the faith of the man on the bed; and in response to *their* faith, he healed the man on the floor with the palsy.

Thus, based upon the word of Scripture, the afflicted one's faith did not seem to be greatly involved in this healing. Rather the key factor pointed out by Jesus, and recorded for our edification by Matthew, Mark and Luke, as being most significant was *the faith* of the friends on the roof looking on.

OBSERVATION:

The man must have had at least a measure of faith, *permissive faith* or *acquiescent faith,* indicated by allowing himself to be carried to a healing service.

=======

Intercessory faith is not the only other kind of faith for healing to be seen in the gospels, there is yet another type.

4

MINISTRY FAITH

The third type of faith for healing recorded in the gospels is *ministry faith.*

Ministry faith for healing is defined as that faith manifested by, or that originates in a third party, other than the sick person, who is praying for the sick person or ministering to him; and may operate independently of the level of faith, if any, possessed by the one needing to be healed.

This type of faith was often manifested by Jesus to those who were lacking in faith of their own. However, identifying it in his case is not always easy, since he so often, generously gave credit for the faith involved to others.

OBSERVATION:

One vital truth is essential. "Faith is a gift lest any man boast," as the Scripture tells us. Therefore, it may only be a matter of semantics as to whether one is given *the gift of healing* or *the gift of faith to be healed.* People have often commented to me that I must have possessed a

23

great deal of faith because I was healed more than twenty years ago of terminal cancer. I usually respond to that question by quoting the aforementioned Scripture. Whether I was the recipient of *a healing* or the recipient of *the gift of faith to be healed* is, I feel, a moot point.

Furthermore, neither gift reveals anything about me. If I were given the gift of a Cadillac, for example, it would tell nothing at all about my character or about me, except of course, that someone cared a great deal for me. It would, on the other hand, tell a great deal about the giver of the gift: that he or she was generous, probably quite wealthy, not selfish, etc. The point is that the gift, while   speaking volumes about the giver, really says noth-ing at all about the recipient.

So it is in the case of a healing. The healing of someone tells us much about the goodness, generosity, compassion, love, power, and virtue of the giver, God, but tells us nothing of the one who is healed, except that he has been greatly favored by God and is now both greatly blessed and physically well!

=======

Certainly the very best example of *ministry faith* to be found in the Scripture is probably that which we observe in Acts 3. The account is recorded there of the man born lame who daily begged alms at the Beautiful Gate of the Temple. Peter   and John were about to enter the Temple at the   hour of prayer, and the beggar seeing them asked alms of them, as Luke graphically records:

> "Now Peter and John went up together into the temple at the hour of prayer, being the ninth hour. And a certain man lame from his mother's womb was carried, whom they laid daily   at the gate of the temple which is

called Beautiful, to ask alms of them that entered into the temple; Who seeing Peter and John about to go into the temple asked an alms. And Peter, fastening his eyes upon him with John, said, "Look on us. And he gave heed unto them, expecting to receive something of them. Then Peter said, Silver and gold have I none; but such as I have give I thee: in the name of Jesus Christ of Nazareth rise up and walk. *And he took him by the right hand, and lifted him up: and immediately his feet and ankle bones received strength.* And he leaping up stood, and walked, and entered with them into the temple, walking, and leaping, and praising God. And all the people saw him walking and praising God: and they knew that it was he which sat for alms at the Beautiful gate of the temple: and they were filled with wonder and amazement at that which had happened unto him. And as the lame man which was healed held Peter and John, all the people ran together unto them in the porch that is called Solomon's, greatly wondering."

Acts 3:1-11

Did you catch it? The man addressed them expecting to receive a piece of money. But Peter surprised him by saying, "Silver and gold have I none; but such as I have, give I thee: in the name of Jesus Christ of Nazareth rise up and walk."

Peter then grabbed the man by the right hand and yanked him up onto his feet. After the man was on his feet, *then* "his feet and ankle bones received strength." Afterwards he went "walking, and leaping, and praising God."

25

There are several important key points in this case. First, the man was directed by Peter to look to the one whose faith was going to be actively involved in the healing (Peter's).

Second, whose faith was it that got the crippled man to his feet? It was Peter's faith! It was Peter's faith that addressed the man; it was Peter's faith that invoked the name of Jesus Christ of Nazareth; and it was Peter's faith that jerked the man up onto his feet.

OBSERVATION:

It *was not* the lame man's faith! He did not say, "I'm going to be healed, I'm going to be healed," or "I claim my healing, I claim my healing," as he struggled to get himself up onto his feet. This is the scenario we might have expected in light of much of today's teaching. No! It was *the faith of Peter, in the name of Jesus,* as Peter himself explained it, in acts 3:16

> "And his name through faith in his name *[Jesus's]* hath made this man strong, whom ye see and know: yea the faith which is by him *[Jesus]* hath given him this perfect soundness in the presence of you all."
>
> (Acts 3:16)

Peter referred twice in this passage to *faith in Jesus* and twice to *His Name.* the fact is clear that it was *the faith of Peter* in the power associated with *the Name of Jesus* that made the man whole. The man's faith is not even mentioned, and probably was non-existent, or Peter would have invoked it. Scripture did not include whether the man even knew who Jesus was, although it is highly unlikely that he would not have heard about Jesus. It is obvious that the man certainly was not a follower of Jesus. Thus it is clear that the man's own faith was not involved in this healing. He was the recipient of a healing bestowed upon him through the operation of *ministry faith*. The healing was ministered to him through the employment of Peter's faith: *his faith in Jesus, faith in Jesus's Name,* and *faith in the healing power available through the use of Jesus's Name.*

==========

5

ELDER, OR BODY FAITH

A fourth category of *healing faith,* involves each of the other three types of healing faith already considered, thus making it a combination of all of the others. Since it involves the whole group and is an operation of a properly functioning body of Christ, I have termed it *elder, or body faith.*

One of the Scriptures most commonly referred to in connection with healing is the passage in the fifth chapter of James:

> "Is any sick among you? Let him call for the elders of the church; and let them pray over him, anointing him with oil in the name of the Lord: And the prayer of faith shall save the sick, and the Lord shall raise him up; and if he have committed sins, they shall be forgiven him. Confess your faults one to another, and pray one for another, that ye may be healed. The effectual fervent prayer of a righteous man availeth much."
>
> James 5:14-16

OBSERVATION:

The wording of this passage indicates sickness to be an unlikely, or uncommon occurrence: "*if any* among you is sick." James doesn't write the words "when," or "as soon as," but *"if."* He apparently doesn't expect this to be the normal condition of believers in the church.

=======

In this passage the Lord, through James, gave specific instructions to his followers about what should be done in the event that someone within the church, the Body, became sick.

[1] *The responsibilities of the person who is sick*

Instructions for the sick person were: "Let him summon the elders." The sick person himself, if able, is expected to summon the elders. Far too often in practice these instructions are reversed. He, the sick person, is to initiate the contact, to seek the aid and ministry of the elders. He is to humble himself and ask them to come to him, confessing coincidentally his need of *the Body.*

This also answers the question often posed to those who express their belief in healing, "Why can't you just go in and empty the hospitals, *if* Jesus really wants to heal everyone?"

The sick person *must ask!* James also wrote in James 4:2, "ye have not *because ye ask not.*"

Man often gets in God's way and messes things up by going to someone too soon, before the individual's own heart has become desperate enough to seek God wholeheartedly for his healing. An illustration from the kitchen might help to see this truth. Bakers know that there is an exact right time to remove a cake from the oven. Take it out too soon and you have a soggy mess; too late and you have a brittle mess. There is a right time to take the cake from the oven. So it is with healing. There is a right time to minister healing! That time I have come to see in most cases is when God has moved upon the heart of that sick person "to summon!"

The Scripture does not say, "Let the elders grab their oil and rush out to the nearest hospital to pray for all who are too sick to outrun them." I am, of course, being facetious, but you see my point. We can only expect God to do what God has Himself said that he would do, and that is to "confirm *his word* with signs and wonders following."

> "And they went forth, and preached every where, the Lord working with them, and confirming the word with signs following."
> Mark 16:20

> "God also bearing them witness, both with signs and wonders, and with divers miracles, and gifts of the Holy Ghost..."
> Hebrews 2:4

Understanding the need to summon aspect explains why so often anointing with oil hasn't seemed to function successfully for many churches. Most churches have never anointed at all; those who do are to be commended for at least attempting it. Out of compassion or misunderstanding of the Scripture, the elders have performed the role of the sick person. God's instructions should be followed, if His promised results are to be expected.

However, if the sick person is unable to summon the elders on his own behalf, it is not at all inappropriate for another close member of the family to do the summoning for him, as parents did in the gospel accounts listed in chapter two on intercessory faith. Strict adherence to a rule can become bondage due to legalism.

All too often I have received calls, usually in the middle of the night, from concerned relatives who request that I go to a hospital and pray for their cousin or uncle. They "know" that sick relative wants me to come, but they have not personally bothered or had the boldness to ask to verify that fact. It didn't take too many long trips to hospitals only to be turned away by the immediate members of the family who didn't want any prayer, or who had their "own minister who does our praying for us," for me to learn that what God said makes an awful lot of sense. Let the sick person, or a member of his immediate family do the summoning.

There is something else that the sick person was instructed to do. He was to "confess his (own) faults to another that he (himself) might be healed." This is often overlooked, but is very important. Many times the sick person must, for example, first confess unforgiveness, which he harbors for another, forgive them, and be cleansed of that unforgiveness before being prayed for, so that he can be healed.

> "And when ye stand praying, forgive, if ye have ought against any: that your father also which is in heaven may forgive you your trespasses."
>
> Mark 11:25

It is extremely important to eliminate unforgiveness and bitterness, as continuing in unforgiveness might become a block to the individual's healing. [1]

[2] *The responsibilities of the elders*

James's instructions for the elders were to anoint the sick person with oil and to pray for him that he might be healed.

[3] *An additional possible function of the elders*

The sick individual by his obedience has exercised *seeking faith.* The elders definitely exercise *intercessory faith* as they pray for, and in behalf of, the sick individual who has summoned them. Finally the elders very often will find themselves also functioning in the area of *ministry faith,* as they endeavor to build up, and encourage the faith of the candidate for healing by relating accounts of other healings and adding their own measure of *ministry faith* to that of the seeker's.

[4] *The responsibilities of all the parties together*

In addition to the elders, the entire body may be involved in praying for the individual's healing. Prayer circles, prayer groups and prayer or healing services, which are often a normal part of fellowships are not only scriptural, but can be very powerful. Perhaps the first prayer circle is recorded in Acts 14 and the apparent raising of the Apostle Paul from the dead:

"And there came thither certain Jews from
Antioch and Iconium, who persuaded the
people, and, having stoned Paul, drew him

----

1. Watch for a forthcoming book by the same author dealing with *Overcoming Blocks To Healing.*

out of the city, supposing he had been dead. Howbeit, as *the disciples stood round about him*, he rose up, and came into the city: and the next day he departed with Barnabas to Derbe."

Acts 14:19,20

Paul admonished believers at Corinth about another important aspect of *Body faith* concerning the observance of the Lord's Supper:

"For he that eateth and drinketh unworthily, eateth and drinketh damnation to himself, not discerning the Lord's body."

I Corinthians 11:29

"That it might be fulfilled which was spoken by Esaias the prophet, saying, himself took our infirmities, and bare our sicknesses."

Matthew 8:17

What is the body to which Paul referred? It is certainly a reference to the physical body of the Lord which "took our infirmities, and bare our sicknesses..." (Mat. 8:17). It is also, I believe, a clear reference to the body of believers, the Body of Christ which gathers to observe the Lord's Supper, the same body which may gather in similar obedience to his instructions *to minister healing in His Name.* Thus the Body of Jesus (believers) makes available the Body of Jesus concerning which, he said, "take, eat: this is my body, which is broken for you," broken for you, not only for sin, in order to provide salvation, but also for sickness in order to provide healing and health!

34

6

MERCY, GRACE, OR MIRACLE

HEALINGS

Two additional categories of supernatural healings bear study. These are not faith healings in the technical sense for they normally involve no faith at all. They are what I describe as *mercy healings*, *grace healings*, or *miracle healings.*

These are those mysterious occurrences when God sovereignly intervenes in the affairs of men and bestows healings without any effort or volitional involvement by the sick individual. We have all read about but can hardly understand the mysterious appearances of Jesus to an individual in his hospital room. A good assumption is that God so desires to heal, that He sometimes steps across the boundaries of time and space and actually visually appears, or somehow makes His presence known or felt, and the individual is made instantly whole.

The best term man has come up with for these occurrences is "miracle," but that is rather generic and inexplicit. It does not differentiate for example between those cases in which no faith is present and those in which faith may play some part. For example, a miracle of this sort happened about ten years ago in St. Louis, Missouri during a Kathryn Kuhlman meeting sponsored by the Full Gospel Business Men's Fellowship, International (FGBMFI) at the former Chase Hotel. Kathryn Kuhlman received a word of knowledge during the meeting that someone wearing a chef's outfit had just been healed.

She dispatched a man to go to the kitchen and see what had happened. The man returned shortly leading a rather surprised looking black man, a cook or chef, wearing a white apron and a tall chef's hat. She asked him what had happened and he replied, "I've had a back condition and have been in constant pain for years. A few moments ago I felt something happening in my back and the pain left me. I've been healed."

Why was the man in the kitchen healed? He was not exercising faith for his own healing. No one else, as far as we know, was praying for the man, but the Lord knew of his need! The Lord knew and acted, healing the man. Perhaps the Lord knew that the only way he would ever be able to reach that black chef was to do it in that miraculous way. It was certainly a tremendous sign or proof of God's supernatural gifts in operation (the word of knowledge listed in I Cor. 12:8) and of his sovereignty and power. It was a faith-builder for the two or three thousand people who saw him and heard the testimony, and for you who may read this account.

But this was a sovereign act of a Sovereign God who wills to, and apparently loves to, demonstrate his love and power in healing. Yet there is apparently some good reason(s) why he does not do it this way all the time. We would all prefer to have Jesus sovereignly deliver our healing to us at home alone in the privacy of our bedroom. However, if he were always to heal in that way there would be no need for the Body of Christ to function as indicated in James 5:14, no need for any faith to be exercised, as no faith was required on the chef's part. There would be no need for us to humble our-selves, to confess our need of the Body of Christ, our need of the prayers of the elders, nor to confess our faults one to another.

Another example of sovereign *grace* or *mercy healing* also occurred in the ministry of Kathryn Kuhlman. She often related cases of drunks who staggered into the lobby of the buildings where her services were taking place, just to get out of the rain or snow...and they were healed. Why? They obviously had no faith, probably didn't even know what was going on inside. Yet they were healed. Kathryn often said she "would never under-stand faith, because many who came to these services with apparent great faith didn't get healed, while many who came with no faith were surprised by being healed." She even said, "Those drunks who got healed, left my services still drunk."

I think it must have been a sobering experience for them to be healed, but she may be right in that they appar-ently left still unchanged spiritually. However, my feel-ing is that in those cases God was extending Himself towards those individuals who would probably never have any other opportunity to come in contact with Him. And so He 'let them have it with both barrels.' He unloaded on them with a miracle because they needed the shock value of the healing more than some of the Christians who were in the audience and already assured of a place in heaven, even if they were to remain unhealed. It may have been that He, in His wisdom knew that the only way He would ever be able to get the attention of those drunks was to heal them.

A variation of this type of healing is what I have described as *spill-over healings*. I have often observed two unusual phenomena associated with the moving of the

Holy Spirit and with healing. One is that the Holy Spirit sometimes seems to move during a healing service in "waves," or categories. That is, in some services he seems to focus on, or choose to specialize in, back problems, or knees, or eye troubles. Other times he seems to zero in on deafness and numerous ears are opened. At still other times there seems to be no discernible pattern to the way he chooses to move, and people may come forward to be healed of a little of everything.

The importance of all this is to be sure to "catch the wave." If, indeed, ears are being healed, and every person who goes forward with hearing problems is having their hearing restored, one with ear trouble would certainly be foolish to hold back. I have experienced evenings when the spirit was moving so freely that I have told the people, "Don't take any pains home with you tonight!" And only the foolish have.

The second unusual phenomenon is described as getting a "spill-over" healing. A doctor friend loves to relate how he was healed of serious sinus trouble while I was praying for someone else with a similar condition. Often times people who understand this principle, simply accept their own healing in our meetings when God is healing someone else of the same condition they have. These, too, may have "caught the wave."

The best advice I can offer one concerning these latter types of healings, is that there is nothing much you can do to prepare yourself for them. However, there is one thing that you *can do* ... and that is to *make yourself available!* Go to the places where these types of miracles are happening. People didn't get healed by avoiding Kathryn Kuhlman services; rather they did get healed by putting themselves out, by forcing themselves to make the journey to her services. Many who would not otherwise have been healed, were healed as a result of going.

So make the decision to force yourself to go where the action is! It is terribly important to remain open to whatever God has for you.

In connection with *grace healing* I will share two accounts of God's grace extended and offered; one that was rejected, one that was accepted.

God often takes a great deal of time to teach us the truths that He wants us to see. God works slowly and deliberately in His process of imparting wisdom to man.

I share two accounts of my attempts to minister to old soldiers, veterans, well into their seventies. Approximately twenty years elapsed between my encountering these two individuals, but considered together they portray several beautiful truths and give a complementary picture of grace, rejected, and accepted. Especially do these accounts illustrate the tremendous role a proper response to God's invitation plays in the salvation or healing process. Remember the clear statement of Scripture:

> "Even so it is not the will of your Father which is in heaven, that one of these little ones should perish."
>
> Matthew 18:14

> "For this is good and acceptable in the sight of God our Saviour; Who will have all men to be saved, and to come unto the knowledge of the truth."
>
> 1 Timothy 2:4

My first ministry to a veteran occurred probably late in 1971 or early in 1972. It happened this way...

39

A Veteran Who Chose to Go To Hell

During the fellowship hour between services at my former Presbyterian church, I was approached by a couple whom I did not know. They said they had a relative who was terminally ill with cancer, as I had been the year before. They asked if I would be willing to go to one of the local Veteran's Hospitals and pray for him to be healed. "We don't know him very well, but we're the only family that Jim has. His prognosis is really bleak. The doctors have said that the cancer is in his throat and they plan to remove a piece of his tongue the day after tomorrow, and fear that they may have to remove both his tongue and his vocal chords. And the worst is, we know that he has no relationship with God; he isn't saved."

I agreed to go, but there was a surprising unwillingness to go, either in my flesh or my spirit, because I really did not want to make this hospital call. I couldn't understand why, but there was a reluctance within me. Usually, I had an eagerness and a feeling of excitement about making hospital calls.

During the 40 minute drive to the hospital, I was still marveling at the fact that I was going in spite of my own wishes. It was clear to me that somehow God was in this hospital visit, because I was mentally dragging my feet all the way. I sensed that I was going strictly out of obedience.

I was also struck by the obvious irony of the fact that the following day in all probability Jim would lose the ability to be able to confess with his mouth Jesus Christ as Lord. I certainly realize, that God certainly wouldn't be hindered from saving one who was inarticulate, or unable to speak, but there was a certain irony and strong impression that this was to be *Jim's last chance!*

When I arrived at the huge hospital, I finally managed to find someone who was able to direct me to the cancer division and to his ward. I found Jim sitting on his bed smoking a cigarette in a six-man ward. I was still fairly new at making hospital calls at that time and mentally winced when I realized that we would have an audience of five additional men listening in on our conversation.

Nevertheless, I began, "Jim, your relatives in Webster Groves asked me to come and see you since I was healed of terminal cancer myself about a year ago." After giving him a brief summary and testimony of what had happened to me, I got right to the purpose for which I had come, "Jim, are you saved?"

"No." He relied in a matter-of-fact fashion.

"Has anyone ever explained salvation to you?" I continued.

"No they haven't," He said seemingly quite open to hear what I had to say.

At that time I don't believe I'd ever encountered a genuine unbeliever or an admittedly unsaved person, and coming from a Presbyterian background, I was not well grounded in salvation scriptures. However, for the next thirty minutes, I explained salvation to Jim. I knew that God was 'really in this ministry' because I was quoting Scriptures to Jim, that I had never learned. I was sitting on a stool in a semi-dazed state (under a heavy anointing, I now recognize) listening in amazement to the absolutely flawless presentation of the salvation message that the Holy Spirit was delivering to this old soldier *out of my mouth!*

> "...take no thought how or what ye shall
> speak: for it shall be given you in that same

41

hour what ye shall speak. For it is not ye that speak, but the Spirit of your Father which speaketh in you."

Matthew 10:19,20

I think I was as awed by the obvious manifestation of God's grace and love extended to this man, as I was by my own almost involuntary role.

When I finished the presentation, as a good salesman, I knew the time had come to 'close the sale.' So I simply asked him, "Jim, wouldn't you like to accept Jesus into your heart now?"

With a glint of hatred flashing in his eyes, he flatly stated, "Nope!"

As soon as I recovered from my shock, naturally expecting him to respond to what God had so beautifully laid out for him, I asked, "Why *wouldn't* you want to accept Him?"

The same cold tone was evident in his voice as he said, "I've made it for seventy-eight years without Him. I'll make it the rest of the way without Him!"

I was stunned by his bluntness and obvious hatred for God, but even more was I shocked by this rejection of an offer that I, personally, knew was extended to him by the very God for whom he was expressing such hatred.

Jim is the only man I ever met *who chose to go to Hell.* I realize that only God sees and knows hearts, and that Jim could possibly have had a conversion at the very last-minute. I believe, God so loved Jim, that He not only sent His Beloved Son to die for him, but He also sent me to him. He had me extend to him another chance, (I'm sure there had been other opportunities that he'd rejected) a death bed chance, to accept His loving offer of Salvation and of Eternal Life, but he rejected this offer too. I remember only too well the mental skid-marks made by my heels all the way to that hospital, while God literally dragged me to that man, whom He so loved. I left the hospital and drove home still in a state of shock at Jim's hatred for, and rejection of, Jesus Christ!

About one month later Jim's relatives approached me at church, told me that he had died, and asked if I'd had a chance to visit with Jim. I replied that I had However, because of Jim's negative response, I did not volunteer more.

"Did he accept the Lord? They asked anxiously.

Regrettably, I had to tell them, "Jim wasn't buying what I was offering."

"We were afraid that was the case," they said. "Jim's heart apparently remained hard right up to the very end. But we do want to thank you for making the trip and for trying."

I found a glorious contrast to this account, however, in what happened with Lester...

A Veteran Who Chose Heaven

There is often, I feel, a direct proportional relationship between the degree of effort, difficulty or pain encountered by the one ministering in delivering ministry to an individual and the degree of blessing received. My favorite story, "Lester, Lester," illustrates this principle.

Nearly twenty years after the experience with Jim, I began experiencing continuing physical symptoms that did not responded to six months of persistent prayer. I dropped fifty pounds in weight and was daily running 103 to 104 degrees of fever. Having become so weak that I could barely get out of bed, I decided to go to a doctor to see if he could help identify the specific thing I should be praying against. After one month of outpatient tests, the doctors were stumped and planning to put me into the hospital for further tests. It was at this time that I received a phone call from a doctor friend who was serving at another Veteran's Hospital in the area.

"Bill, I know how sick you have been and I hate to ask...I know you are too sick to make a hospital call but would you make a telephone call to a man over here in our cancer ward who is dying and needs salvation? He is so far gone that his skin has begun to turn black. His lips have turned black, as well as his extremities. He has three kinds of cancer, plus emphysema and we're giving him ninety pills per day. But realistically he won't live out the week."

Dr. Waggoner paused for a breath and then continued. "The worst of it is that Lester isn't saved. Do you think you could call him, and pray for salvation with him over the phone?"

My friend is a member of our little fellowship and I knew that he was perfectly capable of explaining salvation.

So I said, "I will call him for you." But then I asked, "Why haven't you just gone ahead and explained salvation to him yourself?"

Dr. Waggoner laughed, "Well, first of all as you know, this is a government hospital and it's against government policy to even discuss religion with a patient. And besides," he chuckled. "I tried to explain it to Lester, but he stopped me and said that he wanted to hear it from a *professional!*"

Then I laughed, too, and replied, "Well I don't know that *I* fill the bill, but I'll go ahead and call him for you. What's his number?"

He gave me the number and I dialed Lester. As I dialed, I was dizzy and the room seemed to be spinning. The Devil was whispering in my ear, "Why are you calling this guy, you're sicker than he is. You may not live long enough to complete the call."[1]

As I rebuked those thoughts, Lester answered. I introduced myself, "This is Bill Banks. Your friend, Dr. Waggoner, asked me to call you..."

Lester cut me off, "Did he tell you what this @!%#&! hospital and the other @!%#&! doctors did to me...they charged me for my medicine when I was out on a pass. They want me to pay for the medicine and I'm a Veteran....etc."

----

1. The source of my physical problem eluded the doctors during my hospital stay for three more months. Then by accident they found that I had a perforated intestine which had been burned by radiation twenty years before and had begun to leak. It was repaired in January, 1989.

There was a gurgling, death-rattle in Lester's chest as he raved on about the injustices which he felt had been done to him. He didn't sound like a very good prospect to me, and I knew I didn't have a lot of strength left anyway, so I interrupted him as soon as he stopped for a breath.

"Dr. Waggoner told me that you weren't sure where you'd go if you were to die." I stated bluntly.

"What's ... that?" He shouted, and I thought he was either offended or might be hard of hearing.

"Dr. Waggoner told me that you weren't sure where you'd go if you were to die." I repeated, and he responded a little more softly, "Well, that's true."

"Then, Lester, let me explain to you what salvation is all about." I suggested.

I was pleasantly surprised when he simply replied, "Okay."

I could tell from his previous conversation that he wasn't going to have the patience to listen to my normal complete explanation of salvation. So I gave the briefest possible outline that I felt would cover the basic points, and then once again, boldly 'made the close,' "Lester, would you like to accept Jesus's offer and invite Him into your heart?"

"Yes, I think I should do that." Lester answered unabashedly.

So I proceeded, "Lester, just pray after me, 'Lord, Jesus...'"

Lester followed my lead, and prayed, "Lord, Jesus..."

I continued and led him in a sinner's prayer. When we finished, I said, "Amen."

Lester said, "Amen."

I then said to him, "Well now, Lester, that's it..."

Lester, still following my lead, said, *"Well now, Lester, that's it..."*

I suddenly realized that I had Lester in a 'repeat mode' and he was continuing to *repeat everything that I said.* Finally to break the impasse, I began speaking as rapidly as I could, so that he was unable to keep up. I then told him that he'd done just fine, had prayed the right prayer and to simply trust Jesus for everything.

As soon as I got off the phone, I called Dr. Waggoner and told him my "Lester, Lester" story. He roared with laughter. I also told him that as a *"professional,"* I wasn't too sure about this case, and asked him to be sure to follow up with Lester. Still laughing, he agreed.

A week later Dr. Waggoner called me and said, "I'm sorry to be so long in getting back to you, but would you like to hear a great blessing?"

I said, "Sure!"

"Today was the first chance, that I have had," he explained, "To check back on Lester. Would you believe it, his color is normal; his skin looks like a newborn baby! He is off all medication. They cannot find a trace of cancer in his body, and the emphysema is gone, too! Isn't that fantastic? Apparently that salvation message 'took' in spite of all his repetition."

A month later, Dr. Waggoner called to also tell me that

Lester had returned to the hospital to turn in his handi-capped-parking permit! Lester received the full package of benefits by accepting the One who by His grace gives all blessings. God truly is a God of surprises, and certainly does do "beyond our ability to even think or ask."

==========

Those of you old enough to remember Kathryn Kuhlman's meetings will recall also that the majority of the testimonies of those who were healed usually sounded something like the following:

"I can't believe it. I am healed!"

"I didn't even ask for a healing for myself; I brought my sick sister!"

"I never expected to be healed myself. I just came along to help with my aunt!"
"I don't know why I came to this meeting, but I got healed!"

Of course, it is also true that many who went in faith were healed. However, if you analyze the preceding typi-cal comments of those who were healed, you are struck by the fact that each of them is, in essence, a confession of not having *any* expectancy, or *faith,* for themselves to be healed.

God is a God of Surprises!

Many of those who attended the miracle services were surprised by receiving unexpected healings for themselves. Scripture speaks of God doing more than we could expect.

"But as it is written, Eye hath not seen, nor

48

ear heard, neither have entered into the heart
of man, the things which God hath prepared
for them that love him."

1 Corinthians 2:9

"Now unto him that is able to do exceeding
abundantly above all that we ask or think,
according to the power that worketh in us."

Ephesians 3:20

Thus, as has been noted, a *miracle healing* may re-
quire no faith on the part of the recipient. These individuals receive an unmerited, grace type healing. Remember all
healings, by definition, are *grace healings,* in that all gifts
from God are unmerited, undeserved, unearned. They are
simply sometimes given as love gifts to those of us who
need them so badly without any conscious effort or faith
being involved. Although it seems very strange to us
and perhaps even unfair, many times unbelievers and
those without faith are the recipients of miracles of healing.

Roxanne Brant, a young woman who had a miracle
ministry very similar to that of Kathryn Kuhlman's, once
shared with me that she felt this type of miracle healing
was primarily an evangelistic medium for the Lord. She
said that less than one in five of those miraculously healed
in her services was a mature believer. The majority, over
80%, were new Christians or what she termed baby
Christians.

Many times people are converted as a result of either
themselves or a member of their family being healed.
Sometimes entire families are drawn into the kingdom
of God because the Lord again lovingly sought for and
invited the poor, the maimed, the halt, and the blind to his
feasting table.

49

"Go out quickly into the streets and lanes of the city, and bring in hither the poor, and the maimed, and the halt, and the blind."

Luke 14:21b

There is a logical aspect to this truth. God, of course, cannot expect faith from an unbeliever. An unbeliever cannot be expected to exercise endurance, patience, or faith as Abraham did, as is noted in Hebrews:

"And so, after he had *patiently endured,* he obtained the promise."

Hebrews 6:15

"For ye have need of *patience,* that, after ye have done the will of God, ye might *receive the promise.*"

Hebrews 10:36

God can expect believers to have faith, to patiently await the fulfillment of his promises. But unbelievers, who do not know the promises God has made, have no faith on which to lean, or to give them the strength to hold on for the fulfillment of the promises. Believers may find that God tests and strengthens their faith by delaying the answer to their requests, which necessitates the exercising of both patience and faith!

Children must grow up in order to become full-fledged sons. During my spiritual infancy, it sometimes seemed as if I could hardly get the prayer out of my mouth before the answer arrived. Then God began to deal with me, as I passed out of the infancy or honey-moon stage of my walk with Him, and he lovingly extended the length of time between the praying of the prayer and the arrival of the answer. This is not unlike what occurs in nature as the mother bird begins to nudge the young birds out of the nest, forcing them to test their own wings. God helps us test the wings of our faith by delaying the answers to prayer. But never forget, for those who remain faithful...

> "...Shall the Sun of righteousness arise with healing in his wings..."
>
> Malachi 4:2

A good point to remember and an important key when attempting to *maintain faith* for healing is: A DELAY IS NOT A NO! Simply because you do not yet have in hand the desired answer to your prayer does not mean that it is not enroute.

Remember the perseverance of Daniel...

7

THE PERSEVERANCE

OF DANIEL

What happened to Daniel is of such importance, that the entire passage should be considered. There is an exceptional revelation contained in this account.

"In the third year of Cyrus king of Persia a thing was revealed unto Daniel, whose name was called Belteshazzar; and the thing was true, but the time appointed was long: and he understood the thing, and had understanding of the vision. In those days I Daniel was mourning three full weeks. I ate no pleasant bread, neither came flesh nor wine in my mouth, neither did I anoint myself at all, till three whole weeks were fulfilled. And in the four and twentieth day of the first month, as I was by the side of the great river, which is Hiddekel; Then I lifted up mine eyes, and looked, and behold a certain man clothed in linen, whose loins were girded with fine gold of Uphaz: His body also was like the beryl, and his face as the appearance of lightning,

and his eyes as lamps of fire, and his arms
and his feet like in colour to polished brass,
and the voice of his words like the voice of a
multitude."

Daniel 10:1-6

The Scripture records that Daniel received a vision but
did not understand the significance of its meaning. Therefore he began to fast, apparently a partial fast eating only
vegetables, avoiding bread, meat and wine. Having per-
sisted in his fast for three weeks, on the twenty first day the
Heavenly Messenger arrived to give Daniel the desired and
prayed for understanding of his vision. However, the
Messenger reveals far more and, I feel, gives a message of
far greater significance. For this Spokesman for heaven, in
whom some see the Son of Man (a theophany[1], cf. Rev
1:13-17), draws back the curtain of heaven and allows a
glimpse beyond that veil into the spiritual realm, permitting
us to comprehend something of what is occurring there.

God's message to Daniel opened with an admonition
which reminds us of Jesus's often repeated phrase, "Fear
not," and then gave a confirmation of God's great love for
Daniel. In the first part of His message, the Messenger
explains to whom He has come, why He has come, what
happened in heaven to cause Him to come, and what delayed His arrival.

"And he said unto me, O Daniel, a man
greatly beloved, understand the words that I
speak unto thee, and stand upright: for *unto
thee am I now sent*. And when he had
spoken this word unto me, I stood trembling.

----

1. A visible manifestion or appearance of God to man.

Then said he unto me, *Fear not, Daniel: for from the first day that thou didst set thine heart to understand, and to chasten thyself before thy God, thy words were heard, and I am come for thy words.* But *the prince of the kingdom of Persia withstood me one and twenty days: but, lo, Michael, one of the chief princes, came to help me*; and I remained there with the kings of Persia. Now I am come to make thee understand what shall befall thy people in the latter days: for yet the vision is for many days."

Daniel 10:11-14

The Messenger's words in this account are one of the few instances in Scripture where the Holy Spirit grants an opportunity to see or to know what is actually occurring in Heaven. In this reference the Messenger's words concerning Daniel inspire tremendous faith in me, and should do so in all who read this passage with understanding.

First, He states that He has come specifically to Daniel. Thus the man, Daniel, is known by name in heaven, to God the Father and to this Messenger. (A reminder that God knows each of us by name). Second, He says that Daniel is "greatly beloved." The reason for his being loved will be considered in connection with his eligibility to be heard. Third, He has come because of Daniel's words and to give him the requested understanding concerning the previous vision. Fourth, He explains what took place in heaven: the very moment that Daniel set his heart to understand, to seek God, and began to pray and fast, his words were heard in heaven and that the Messenger was dispatched because of Daniel's prayers. Finally, fifth, although the Messenger was dispatched immediately, the very day that Daniel began to pray and seek God, He was delayed by the warring actions of the prince of the Kingdom of Persia.

If you are trusting God for something, and are attempting to persevere, trusting God, but the thing has not yet been provided, continue persevering for that is the message of Daniel's experience. It blesses us to know that *the very moment that Daniel prayed his prayer, the prayer was heard, and, in essence, the wheels in heaven were immediately set in motion to deliver the answer to his request.*

The Heavenly Messenger was dispatched the very moment that Daniel prayed. So, we can know that when we pray for something, the prayer has been heard and the answer is enroute... even if we do not yet see any evidence to that effect. This makes it possible for us to understand the intent of Jesus' statement in Mark.

> "Therefore I say unto you, What things soever ye desire, *when ye pray,* believe that ye receive them, and ye shall have them."
> Mark 11:23b,24

However, we note that the Messenger, and the answer to his prayer, did not arrive when he prayed, but three weeks later. The Messenger explained that He was delayed for twenty-one days by satanic forces. But do not overlook the fact: the very moment that the prayer was prayed - the answer was dispatched.

Unlike Daniel, I might have given up after one week of fasting if the answer to my prayer had not arrived. I would probably have given up on my fast and concluded, "I must have missed God this time. It must not have been His will to grant my prayer. I must have either failed God in some way, or somehow I must not be eligible."

What does the Holy Spirit reveal concerning the part Daniel played in bringing about this visitation and answer to his prayer? I see four major points, which can aid us both in waging spiritual warfare, and in praying with power.

1. Daniel knew that God was there: that God had heard his prayer and that God was going to answer his prayer. He believed that God would answer his prayer. Similarly, men of faith in the past have believed with singleness of heart that God would answer their prayers. Their hearts were fixed, awaiting God to do that which God said He would do; to answer their prayers, or to do that which they *knew God could perform.*

2. If Daniel had doubts, he resisted and overcame those doubts.

3. Daniel began a fast and continued both fasting and believing, until his answer arrived.

4. The basis for Daniel's prayer being answered was that Daniel had *set his heart to understand,* had determined to chasten himself, to fast, until he got his answer. As a result, of these conditions being met, *"I am come for thy words."*

Daniel "set his heart." He had fixed his heart, as the Psalmist said,

> "...the righteous shall be in everlasting remembrance. He shall not be afraid of evil tidings: *his heart is fixed,* trusting in the Lord."
>
> Psalm 112:6,7

Daniel had set his will to receive from God, and the answer came! "I am come *for your words,"* your words move God. The power of life and death are in your tongue, indeed, if your words in prayer can cause God to take notice of them and to dispatch angels in answer to your words.

If you have prayed and your answer hasn't yet come... *remember Daniel!*

Daniel's experience with answered prayer is reminiscent of what happened to Hezekiah when he was sick unto death, and God sent His prophet, Isaiah, unto him with a message.[1]

"In those days was Hezekiah sick unto death. And Isaiah the prophet the son of Amoz came unto him, and said unto him, Thus saith the Lord, Set thine house in order: for thou shalt die, and not live.
Then Hezekiah turned his face toward the wall, and prayed unto the Lord,
And said, Remember now, O Lord, I beseech thee, how I have walked before thee in truth and with a perfect heart, and have done that which is good in thy sight. And Hezekiah wept sore."

Isaiah 38:1-3

"And it came to pass, afore Isaiah was gone out into the middle court, that the word of the Lord came to him, saying,
Turn again, and tell Hezekiah the captain of my people, Thus saith the Lord, the God of David thy father, I have heard thy prayer,

----

1. The two accounts from Isaiah and 2 Kings have been combined in order to present certain details uniquely recorded in each.

I have seen thy tears: behold, I will heal
thee: on the third day thou shalt go up unto
the house of the Lord.
    And I will add unto thy days fifteen
years..."

2 Kings 20:4-6a

Because Hezekiah repented after receiving his 'death
sentence' from the Lord, God told Isaiah to go back and tell
him, "I have heard thy prayer and I have seen thy tears."
God heard the repentant prayer of that rebellious king and
granted him another fifteen years of life.

Just as in Daniel's experience, the very moment that
Hezekiah's prayer was uttered, it was heard and the answer
dispatched. In fact, before Isaiah had even reached the
middle court of Hezekiah's palace, after delivering God's
first message to him, God sent His messenger, Isaiah this
time, back to Hezekiah with the answer to his prayer.

The principle clearly granted to us in these two cases
of answered prayer is that *the very moment a prayer is
uttered on earth by any eligible child of God, it is heard,
and the answer dispatched.*

I qualify this principle to the extent that it *only pertains
to those prayers prayed in accordance with the will of God.*
This fact is made clear in the New Testament restatement
of this same principle in 1 John.

"And this is the confidence that we have in
him, that, if we *ask any thing according to
his will,* he heareth us: And if we know that
he hear us, whatsoever we ask, we know that
we have the petitions that we desired of
him."

1 John 5:14,15

59

Why didn't the answer come sooner for Daniel? Why do answers not come sooner for you and for me? Who prevented it? This, I feel, is the great blessing for us in this passage, for it reveals to us the source of opposition.

It also explains why Daniel's answer, and the answers to prayers prayed today, are often delayed - because of satanic opposition! Satan desires to convince us that God neither hears nor will answer our prayers. He wants us to despair and to give up on God. If we lose heart (faith), cease to persevere, we may miss out on the blessings already enroute to us!

Obviously no earthly prince could have withstood or delayed such a messenger from Heaven's Throne. Certainly not an angelic messenger of the level of Archangel, for those who believe this to be Gabriel, or the Son of God, for those who see this as a theophany. This was obviously a *satanic,* or *demonic prince* over the principality or country of Persia. No mere earthly prince or even king, could have held back Heaven's Messenger.

The messenger explains that he was withstood twenty-one days by the prince of Persia, until he was able to summon reinforcements under a prince of Heaven, the Archangel Michael. With the aid of Michael (and the implied angelic forces under his direction) Heaven's Messenger battled through and was able to deliver the answer to Daniel's prayer.

> "For we wrestle not against flesh and blood, but against principalities [*areas ruled by a prince*], against powers, against the rulers of the darkness of this world, against spiritual wickedness in high places."
>
> Ephesians 6:12

The resistance in the demonic realm was not defeated, until a two-pronged battle was waged and won. Daniel battled in the earthly plain by his fasting and persevering, continuing to believe God: in the heavenly or supernatural realm, the Messenger with the aid of Michael battled through the satanic opposition. In a sense they pushed their way through from above, and Daniel pulled them through from this dimension by his faithfulness and perseverance.

"Then said he, Knowest thou wherefore I come unto thee? and now will I return to fight with the prince of Persia: and when I am gone forth, lo, the prince of Grecia shall come. But I will show thee that which is noted in the scripture of truth: and there is none that holdeth with me in these things, but Michael your prince."

Daniel 10:20-21

The Messenger says upon leaving that He is going back to continue his battle with the prince of Persia. Why? Because, I am convinced, that there were other prayers of unrecorded faithful believers pending, and He was going to continue battling so that He might deliver answers to their prayers also!

God cares about your problems! And wants you to know Him fully, have faith in Him, and to be able to pray to Him in faith.

8

CLOSING THOUGHTS FOR

THOSE NOT HEALED (*YET*)!

In closing let me offer a few thoughts for those who may have attended a miracle service, such as those of Kathryn Kuhlman or Benny Hinn, and have come away without receiving a healing there, as I have. [1]

1.) You are blessed to have seen the power of God demonstrated. That demonstration of His power should have greatly encouraged you and your own faith.

2.) Remember, the fact that you aren't healed YET, does not mean that your healing is not enroute to you. A DELAY IS NOT A NO!

3.) You have probably seen at the crusade many serious needs in the great crowd. Many of those needs seemed greater than your own, and you may have either

----

1. The author was not healed when he attended a Kathryn Kuhlman meeting in 1970, but his faith was greatly enhanced by what he saw there. He was subsequently healed of terminal cancer about six months later. The story is told in the book *Alive Again!*

thought or felt, "God, I'm not really as bad off as some of these other people. They need your healing touch even more than I do. Please heal them."

Your compassion is to be commended, however the theology that usually goes along with it, is wrong. Satan would have you believe that it is more important for *them* to be healed, than for you and therefore, only the others will be healed. That is another of Satan's lies.

Satan often uses this honest compassion against you as a block to your faith, leading you to think, "They need it more than I do: heal them (*instead of me*)!" Thus your personal faith to be healed is effectively eroded.

Remember another great truth given to me by a revelation from the Holy Spirit, God is all sufficient. We aren't going to cause a power failure in heaven if He heals *both* them and us! Grasp this fact: *we will not dim the lights in Heaven by having God heal both you and all those other needy individuals!* His grace and power are more than sufficient to heal every person in that huge crowd!

4.) Remember also that God's *power, compassion, mercy* and *His will to heal you* has not changed just because that particular miracle service is over!

5.) Do not forget the difference between *a miracle* and *a healing*. A miracle happens in the twinkling of an eye. A healing takes time. This truth is confirmed in the words of Jesus, Himself. He said "...believers *shall* lay hands on the sick and they *shall recover*." A healing does take time: "shall" implies future action; to "recover" also implies a future action. It is quite possible that your *healing* has already begun!

6.) Do not let your present discouragement cause you to give up on God; He hasn't given up on you!

7.) To restate a thought presented in the sixth paragraph of this section: if every person who needed to be healed could simply go to a Benny Hinn Miracle Crusade and get his miracle, there would no longer be any need for James 5:14, the elders, or the anointing with oil.

Remember, the <u>only</u> Scriptural prescription for a sick or afflicted Christian *is for him to summon the elders* in accordance with the passage in James.

Having seen a miracle crusade, having had your faith in God's will to heal increased, faith in His tremendous awe-inspiring power enhanced, now go in the strength of your re-charged faith to your own elders, or seek out those in your city who can pray with you, in faith, believing for your healing!

SOME OF MY FAVORITE
HEALING SCRIPTURES

The Word of God is powerful! It alone can create faith and strengthen the believer. The following Scriptures are some by which I have been particularly blessed. These can build your faith, can be used by you to make your own stand upon, can become your personalized confession, or can also be used offensively against the enemy as you stand in faith, believing, and persevering for your healing!

"My son, attend to my words; incline thine ear unto my sayings. Let them not depart from thine eyes; keep them in the midst of thine heart. For they are life unto those that find them, and health to all their flesh."

Prov. 4:20-22

"...If thou wilt diligently hearken to the voice of the Lord thy God, and wilt do that which is right in his sight, and wilt give ear to his commandments, and keep all his statutes, I will put none of these diseases upon thee, which I have brought upon the Egyptians: for I am the Lord that healeth thee."

Exodus 15:26

"Heal me, O Lord, and I shall be healed; save me, and I shall be saved: for thou art my praise."

Jeremiah 17:14

"Bless the Lord, O my soul: and all that is within me, bless his holy name. Bless the Lord, O my soul, and forget not all his benefits: Who forgiveth all thine iniquities; who healeth all thy diseases..."

Psalms 103:1-3

"He sent his word, and healed them, and delivered them from their destructions."

Psalms 107:20

"And it came to pass, when he was in a certain city, behold a man full of leprosy: who seeing Jesus fell on his face, and besought him, saying, Lord, if thou wilt, thou canst make me clean. And he put forth his hand, and touched him, saying, I will: be thou clean. And immediately the leprosy departed from him."

Luke 5:12,13

"I will praise thee; for I am fearfully and wonderfully made: marvellous are thy works; and that my soul knoweth right well."

Psalms 139:14

"The blind receive their sight, and the lame walk, the lepers are cleansed, and the deaf hear, the dead are raised up, and the poor have the gospel preached to them."

Matthew 11:5

And all things, whatsoever ye shall ask in prayer, believing, ye shall receive."

Matthew 21:22

"Beloved, I wish above all things that thou mayest prosper and be in health, even as thy soul prospereth."

3 John 1:2

"Even so it is not the will of your Father which is in heaven, that one of these little ones should perish."

Matthew 18:14

"Surely he hath borne our griefs, and carried our sorrows: yet we did esteem him stricken, smitten of God, and afflicted. But he was wounded for our transgressions, he was bruised for our iniquities: the chastisement of our peace was upon him; and with his stripes we are healed."

Isaiah 53:4,5

"Who his own self bare our sins in his own body on the tree, that we, being dead to sins, should live unto righteousness: by whose stripes ye were healed."

1 Peter 2:24

"When the even was come, they brought unto him many that were possessed with devils: and he cast out the spirits with his word, and healed all that were sick: That it might be fulfilled which was spoken by

Esaias the prophet, saying, Himself took our infirmities, and bare our sicknesses."

Matthew 8:16-17

"And Jesus went forth, and saw a great multitude, and was moved with compassion toward them, and he healed their sick."

Matthew 14:14

"...they should see with their eyes and hear with their ears, and should understand with their heart, and should be converted, and I should heal them."

Matthew 13:15b

"And all things, whatsoever ye shall ask in prayer, believing, ye shall receive."

Matthew 21:22

"And great multitudes followed him; and he healed them there."

Matthew 19:2

"...but speak the word only, and my servant shall be healed."

Matthew 8:8

"...and as many as touched were made perfectly whole."

Matthew 14:35-36

"And the Lord will take away from thee all sickness, and will put none of the evil diseases of Egypt, which thou knowest, upon upon thee..."

Deuteronomy 7:15a

> "And Jesus went about all the cities and villages, teaching in their synagogues, and preaching the gospel of the kingdom, and healing every sickness and every disease among the people. But when he saw the multitudes, he was moved with compassion on them, because they fainted, and were scattered abroad, as sheep having no shepherd. Then saith he unto his disciples, The harvest truly is plenteous, but the labourers are few; Pray ye therefore the Lord of the harvest, that he will send forth labourers into his harvest."
>
> Matthew 9:35-38

What kind of laborers, or workers, was it that Jesus was praying the Father to send forth into the harvest fields? He was praying for those who would be shepherds for the sheep, certainly. But even more to the point He was praying for workers that would minister to those sheep toward whom He felt compassion in the same way that He would minister to them if He were with them, Himself: He was praying for MEN to minister to His sheep the HEALING and DELIVERANCE which they so greatly needed.

By way of confirmation of this analysis note the five instances of ministry in the preceding verses of the ninth chapter: He healed the man with palsy; He healed the woman with the flow of blood, raised Jairus's daughter: He healed two blind men, and finally He cast a demon out of a dumb man. Further confirmation is to be seen in the fact that Jesus began answering His own prayer in the very next verse, the first verse of Chapter 10.

> "And when he had called unto him his twelve disciples, he gave them power against unclean spirits, to cast them out, and to heal all manner of sickness and all manner of disease."
>
> Matthew 10:1

71

Powerful Help on Cassette

Are You Saved? Have You Been BORN AGAIN?
Do you even know for sure what is meant by these
questions?

If not, we strongly recommend that you send for
the tape
  HOW TO BE SAVED, or BORN AGAIN!

To receive this informative tape, which can change
your life . . . just as it has for thousands of others,
when they have heard the message contained on
the tapes and responded to it. . . .

  Simply send your name and address along with
$5.00 to cover all costs to:

IMPACT BOOKS, INC.
137 W. Jefferson
Kirkwood, MO 63122

NOTE: If you honestly cannot afford to pay for the tape, we will
send it to you free of charge.

POWERFUL NEW BOOK
BY SAME AUTHOR . . .

This new book is unique because it offers real help for the suffering women who have already had abortions. This book is full of GOOD NEWS!

It shows how to minister to them, or may be used by the women themselves as it contains simple steps to self-ministry.

Millions of women **have had abortions**: every one of them is a potential candidate for the type of ministry presented in this book. Every minister, every counsellor, every Christian should be familiar with these truths which can set people free.

$5.95 + $1.00 Shipping/Handling

IMPACT BOOKS, INC.
137 W. Jefferson, Kirkwood, Mo. 63122

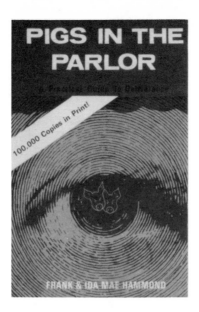

Bestseller I I

PIGS IN THE
PARLOR $5.95

If you *really believe* JESUS delivered people from evil spirits . . . Then you owe it to yourself to read this book! Learn that it *still happens today!*

This book contains a wealth of practical information for the person **interested in, planning to engage in,** or actively engaged in the ministry of deliverance.

It is a PRACTICAL HANDBOOK, offering valuable guidance as to determining . . .

> • HOW DEMONS ENTER • IF DELIVERANCE IS NEEDED • HOW DELIVERANCE IS ACCOMPLISHED FOR OTHERS AND SELF • HOW TO RETAIN DELIVERANCE • GROUPINGS OF DEMONS (listing those demons that are often found together).

The book also includes a chapter presenting a revelation on the problems of **SCHIZOPHRENIA** which could well revolutionize the way this subject has been traditionally viewed by the medical profession!

A BLOOD COVENANT
IS THE MOST
SOLEMN, BINDING AGREEMENT POSSIBLE
BETWEEN TWO PARTIES.

Perhaps one of the least understood, and yet most important and relevant factors necessary for an appreciation of the series of covenants and covenant relationships that our God has chosen to employ in His dealings with man, is the concept of the BLOOD COVENANT!

In this volume which has been "sold out," and "unavailable" for generations, lies truth which has blessed and will continue to bless every pastor, teacher, every serious Christian desiring to "go on with God."

Andrew Murray stated it beautifully years ago, when he said that if we were to but grasp the full knowledge of what God desires to do for us and understood the nature of His promises, it would "make the Covenant the very gate of heaven! May the Holy Spirit give us some vision of its glory."

$8.95

BEST SELLERS FROM
IMPACT BOOKS
137 W. Jefferson, Kirkwood, MO 63122

BOOKS _____

____ ALIVE AGAIN	4.95	____ MIRACLE BUS TO THE SHRINE 2.95

____ ALIVE AGAIN — 4.95
____ A LOVE STORY — 1.25
____ DECISION TO DISCIPLESHIP — 1.25
____ GOLD FROM GOLGOTHA — 1.50
____ GREATER WORKS SHALL YE DO — 2.95
____ HOW TO HEAR GOD SPEAK — 1.50
____ IS FAITH REQUIRED FOR YOUR MIRACLE — 2.95
____ KINGDOM LIVING — 4.95
____ MINISTERING TO THE LORD — 4.50
____ MINISTERING TO ABORTION'S AFTERMATH — 3.95

____ MIRACLE BUS TO THE SHRINE — 2.95
____ MY PERSONAL PENTECOST — 1.25
____ PIGS IN THE PARLOR — 5.95
POWER FOR DELIVERANCE SERIES:
____ SONGS OF DELIVERANCE — 5.95
____ DELIVERANCE FROM FAT — 5.95
____ DELIVERANCE FOR CHILDREN — 5.95
____ THE BLOOD COVENANT — 5.95
____ TRIAL BY FIRE — 3.50
____ THE HEAVENS DECLARE — 6.95

MUSIC & SONG BOOKS _____

____ DELUXE GUITAR PRAISE BOOK — 3.95
____ FAVORITE HYMNS ARR. FOR CLASSICAL GUITAR — 3.95
____ FAVORITE HYMNS ARR. FOR PIANO — 3.95
____ GOSPEL BANJO — 3.95
____ GUITAR CHRISTMAS CAROLS — 2.95
____ GUITAR HYMNAL — 3.95
____ JESUS SONGS! — 3.95
____ GOSPEL GUITAR — 3.95
____ HYMNS FOR DULCIMER — 4.95
____ LITURGICAL GUITARIST — 15.00
____ ONE WAY SONGBOOK — 3.95
____ SACRED GUITARIST — 3.95
____ SACRED ORGANIST — 3.95

____ SACRED PIANIST — 3.95
____ "SIGNS SHALL FOLLOW" SONG BOOK — 3.95
____ SPIRIT FILLED SONGS — 3.95
____ CHILDREN'S GUITAR HYMNAL — 2.95
____ HYMNS FOR AUTOHARP — 4.95
____ HYMNS FOR CLASSICAL GUITAR FOSTER — 4.95
____ MORE HYMNS FOR CLASSIC GUITAR-FOSTER — 4.95
____ SONGS OF CHRISTMAS FOR AUTOHARP — 2.50
____ LITURGICAL GUITARIST (CASS.) — 9.95
____ FAMILY HYMN BOOK — 6.95
____ HYMNS FOR HARMONICA — 5.95

Bill Banks.
Terminal Cancer.
48 hours to live.
Miraculously
healed!

Name _____

Address _____

_____

For your convenience, you may use
either MasterCard or Visa.

Mastercard No. _____

Visa No. _____

Expiration Date _____

FOR ADDITIONAL COPIES WRITE:

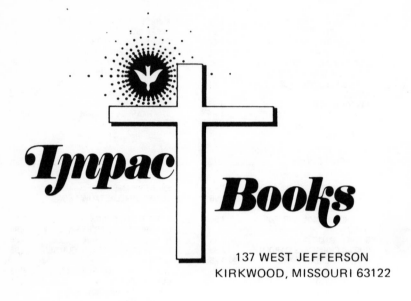

137 WEST JEFFERSON
KIRKWOOD, MISSOURI 63122

AVAILABLE AT YOUR LOCAL BOOKSTORE, OR YOU MAY
ORDER DIRECTLY. Toll-Free, order-line only M/C, DISC,
or VISA 1-800-451-2708.